DATE DUE

OFFICIALLY DISCARDED

D1558152

This book was donated by the
Siskiyou Arts Council
Gallery & Cultural Center

www.SiskiyouArtsCouncil.org

418 N Mt. Shasta Blvd.
938-0130

THE WELL VERSED invite comments from readers. To offer feedback, inquire about membership and sponsorship, or to order books, please contact us.

THE WELL VERSED
c/o Lily Gebhart, Secretary
301 East Lake Street
Mount Shasta, CA. 96067

We extend special thanks to the following members for their enthusiasm, time and energy:

Ashalyn, Art Director
Vicky Ferrasci, Treasurer
Lily Gebhart, Secretary and Editor
Jane Hoffman, Artistic/Technical Consultant
Michael McClure, Artistic Consultant/Distributions
Linda Neal, Submissions Coordinator
Prem RajaBaba, Photographer/Productions Coordinator

And to Wilem Vonk and Peggy Loucks, at Has Beans Coffee Roasterie and Cafe, 1011 S. Mt. Shasta Blvd., for hosting meetings of THE WELL VERSED, and opening their doors to local poets for readings-aloud.

All proceeds from sales of this book will fund future anthologies of THE WELL VERSED.

THE INKWELL
By Vicky Ferrasci

A spot of ink upon
The page so white
Nourished by memories,
Inner dreams, and hopes;
It grows into so much more.

Enveloped by the spirit of unity
The small spot grows into words,
Reflections of deep thought,
An inner well of knowledge.

We are joined by a desire
To be heard, to listen,
To speak of memories within,
Or just let feelings out.

Together the words flow freely,
As if drawn from a never-ending source
We dip our pens together and
The ideas pour forth, for we are
An overflowing inkwell.

PREFACE

Mount Shasta has always drawn people who march to the beat of a drum with a more subtle rhythm than most. Nowhere is this more apparent than in the fine writing produced by so many talented people in this unique area.

The profound, multi-level expression of the local poets is the epitomy of this. Poetry has always been the "Language of the Gods" in that thoughts and feelings go directly from the mind of writer to reader without the limitations of strict word definitions or interpretations.

Poetry needs to be experienced with a quiet mind...reading each verse at least three times to allow the levels of meaning to rise from within. Experienced in this way, the magic of these words will be truly apparent, as special for you as it has been for me.

R. L. S.
Mount Shasta, California
July 1996

vi

TABLE OF CONTENTS

INTRODUCTION

Through the enthusiasm generated by Lily Gebhart (pen name, Lily Vallerey), a gathering of local poets came together. THE WELL VERSED is a guild of talented and motivated writers. We continue to grow in scope and vision, creating an outlet for writing, performing, and sharing the abundant talent in this area.

Along the mysterious path of our creative process, this anthology has come to rest in your hands. You hold the work of all ages, of diverse styles, and of concepts that delve deep within the psyche, or soar up into the stars...that explore the manifestations of nature, the splendor of love, the unfolding of mystical experiences, the pain of memory and growth, or the simple elegance of a momentary insight. As you travel with your eyes, your voices, your hearts and minds the journeys we share with you on these pages, you are invited to the experience of your own unique response -- a chuckle, a tear, a new dream, an urge to pick up a pen and contribute your own verse -- all of these, and more. We've turned ourselves inside out, and set forth the inner splendor of our creativity to share with you.

The dream is never static. It is our hope that this is the first volume of many anthologies. The outcome rests with the enjoyment and support of our families, friends, readers, and appreciators of the arts within and beyond the range of the master sentinel, Mount Shasta. Your response is welcome, for it is part of the song that courses through us and emerges in words of THE WELL VERSED.

MISSION STATEMENT: To assist aspiring local poets to polish, perform and publish their creations with an attitude of encouragement and celebration in the ongoing process of mastering their art.

"Touched by poetry,
language is more fully language
and at the same time,
it is no longer language: it is a poem."

-- Octavio Paz

Ashalyn doesn't write poetry, she simply records it, as given to her by nature spirits and the spirit of the Earth Mother. When she lovingly acknowledges the spirits, they communicate with her in poetic and story form about "their views of life on Earth and beyond." As a spiritual counselor and healer, Ashalyn has been communing with Spirit for over 20 years. She "accidentally" discovered her poetic gift in 1990 while asking the Earth Mother to help her release anger. In the process, the rocks she was lying on spoke to her, saying: "Time immemorial runs through our veins. We see. We see. Ask us for that which you seek. We see. We see." Her upcoming book, *Earth Speaks: Inspirational Messages from the Nature Spirits*, is a collection of this poetry and an explanation of our symbiotic relationship with nature spirits in the magnificent Dance of Life.

MOUNTAIN'S OFFER
from Mount Shasta

Many travelers come my way
hoping to see life's wonders in stone.
Mountains hold mysteries
way beyond the imaginations
of well-meaning seekers of Light.

Within this mountain rests wisdom...
wisdom given freely to those who seek.
Walk upon my pathways
and I shall give you freedom
from worries, cares, and fears
burdening you on this
your great Earth Walk.

I offer solace.
I offer hope.
I offer visions
of much more to come.
I am here to help Man see
the folly of his ways
as compared to the purposeful magic
of Nature.
I find within Man
a quality that greatly pleases me...
a quality of hope
not far beneath the surface of
depression and hopelessness.
This quality of hope
is what I uncover
as I gently encourage Man
to try once more
to walk in the footsteps
of the Father.

If you can make it up to my lofty pinnacles
I will show you the purpose
of life upon this planet.
I will show you the meaning of Love
as it burns within the heart of Man...
love much greater than any seen
through eyes of hopelessness and fear.

Love upon this mountain
grows and grows
until there is nothing more
than Love itself,
complete and whole,
everywhere,
and in everything.

FULL MOON IN LIBRA
(written in full moon's light)

Full moon shines down
so brightly on me,
lighting each movement I make.
Crystal clear evening
no hint of a wind,
So quiet
you can hear yourself breathe.

My soul lights up
in full moon's rays.
It wants to express
and be seen at its best.
Wise men marvel
at moon's glorious grace,
guilding the sky
with its sheen.

Wise man honors moon phases,
shifting tides and emotions,
moon phases
that honor Earth's cycles,
from beginning to end,
and again.

Full moon inspires lovers
bringing them to heights
not yet met.
Wandering souls quiver
under moon's influence.
Unanswered questions surface,
drawing out earnest life prayers.

Full moon speaks
of full self expression
not leaving out one valuable piece
of its precious material.

3

Full moon makes itself known
to all those who greet
the night sky.
"Come listen to me,
and I will reflect
your deepest rememberings."

DANCE OF THE ICE FAIRIES
at Faery Falls in February

Ice forms captivate Nature's movements.
Encased in glass-like structures
the Mother is frozen
in a moment's breath.

Painting landscapes in still form,
the Ice Fairies prance
from branch to branch,
droplet to droplet,
arranging their subjects
in the most beautiful pose
before Ice hardens them
in their final stone-like form.
Here they are captured
until Sunlight's warming glow
releases them once more
to blow gracefully with the breeze
and sprout Spring growth at will.

Jumping from rock to rock
the Ice Fairies paint magical landscapes
with textures and designs
fit for Kings and Queens...
no two alike, mind you,
from year to year,
month to month,
day to day
these landscapes
take on a life of their own
in their forced stillness.

4

Snowflakes fall upon them
adding their creative input
to those silent sculptures,
building and building on them
until some become so heavy
they snap under the weight
of their icy cold cells.

Yes, Mother Nature's busy
in all four seasons
captivating Man's fancy
with a creative twinkle
in Her loving eye...
offering beauties galore
to tease the senses...
here and now,
and forever more!

WATERFALL'S RAPTURE
by Faery Falls in May

I am the expression of Love in its glory.
Full figured I stand as I explode in mid-leap.
Oxygen mixed with hydrogen
pummels forth in radiant bliss
as I represent fullness that's overflowing.

Put yourself inside a single drop of me
as we wander joyously,
splashing wildly forth.
Feel the explosions of glee
as we blast forth into infinite space...
freedom personified as water falls...
pushed forth by a force
much grander than myself...
driven wildly by gravity's pull
and snow melt's push.

Not thinking twice about which way I splash,
just splashing forth
in the rapture of *this* moment
a mere drop in Creation's landscape
but fully perfected within my own bliss.

Rapture, sweet rapture,
carries me forth each day...
offering nothing but jubilance,
passion and joy!
May I be a witness to that state...
an on-going example
of rapture in liquid form
beckoning you to follow.

Bliss tells me you need a lift.
Bliss says you feel hollow.
Bliss says, "Lift her up with us now,
and encourage her play!"
Heavy thoughts weigh one down...
heavy thoughts hamper play.
Give them to me one at a time
and I will explode them in an instant.

Put your emotional trash in me
and allow me to unburden you
for I have the capacity to handle great storms,
whether snow melt water
or emotional tears.

So share your sorrows with me
and together we can change the world
from a place of sorrow and grief
to a place of ecstatic communion with all life
as it presents itself to you!

THE WHITE GIANT

The first snow of winter,
It gets whiter by the day.
You ponder its majesty
Then the snow turns to rain.
The fallen snow starts to recede,
The sun makes the white coat shine.
Canyons form from melting snow
Announcing summertime.
Snow vanishes as quickly as it came.
The streams begin to flow.
Birds sing once again
As trees shake off their snow.

FIRST RAYS OF LIGHT AT DAWN

How beautiful the sun's rays are
On a cool winter morning,
Gleaming at dawn's early light.
As the light slowly glistens
Off the pictures on the wall,
Opening the darkness of the night.
A new day is dawning
As the light is reborn
Announcing the coming of morn.
Light gleaming through icicles,
As if captured in crystal,
Reflecting the day that is born.

FREDERICK BENTON

Free-lance writer; retired CDF Ranger.

SNOW GEESE, NORTH OF SACRAMENTO

Each Fall they arrive--
a celebration of wings,
their ancient clamoring rich
with distance and mystery.
They have come far, unerringly,
to their Winter home.
Whirling like wind-driven
flakes of powder snow
beneath lead-gray skies,
the great, milling flocks
brim the smoke-hazed valley
with heartbreaking cries.

Listen: they come
from beyond the north wind,
through sunshine and storm,
streaming south over moonlit ranges,
high in the bitter cold,
wave upon rippling wave,
shimmering like northern lights.
Listen: their music
is a gift to each of us,
their wildness is a truth
which haunts our dreams
like winter--like love.

REFLECTION

Heart Lake surprises us with her shape,
She's such a loving thing;
That when we rest upon her shores
She makes our own heart sing.
The fairies dance across her skin,
Coaxing magic from the deep;
The light then rises to the top;
The brightness makes us weep.
And when she says, "It's time to go...
You've drank enough of me,"
We take home a new light-ness;
Her heart has set ours free.

THE EMPTY

It seems there's not enough of me,
I'm like the jam-less jar;
Your knife clinks 'round inside my shell...
No sweetness found so far.
Perhaps a little stuck under the swell
Of my being where the lid screws on?
But fruitless search reveals the truth...
Even the scent is gone.
So, spread your toast with someone else,
And toss me in the bin,
Where I'll recycle what's left of me,
And start all over again.

THE GARDEN

She bends her head down to the ground
And digs her fingers in the dirt;
She comes alive with tears of joy
Which paint a landscape on her shirt.
The earth has saved her, once again,
From all the days delivered;
Her weeping waters what she grows;
Now blooms what might have withered.

SUSAN F. CLOUSER

THE SENTINEL

Oh, Mount Shasta,
There you are,
Wishing high
Upon a star;
Cradling the village
In your arms;
Enticing hikers
With your charms;
Standing proud,
For all to see,
In quiet moments
Of reverie;
Then singing out
Your song of hope
At times we earthlings
Need it most.
Your strength,
Your snow,
Your lofty peak
Soothe the soul
Of all who seek;
And when we're pulled
Away from you,
It's reasoned that
Your work is through.

POETRY

Where do you come from,
Little verse 'o mine?

I swept you up
From off the floor
In just the nick 'o time.

Who dropped this
Little morsel?
(From which I now partake)

You're just a crumb
From up above;

I'd love to see the cake!

THE TINY GARDENER

Abaji came to town
With a flower and a sword,
And dug up my calloused heart.
He planted his seedling
There within,
Then gave it a kiss for good start.
His tiny fingers
Pull the weeds
We grownups tend to let go;
You see,
He remembers how things work.
He knows what makes us grow.
He waters daily
With his song,
And feeds with a smile so bright.
It's this tiny gardener
Who nurtures me,
And fills my days with delight.

10

A.C . CONLAN

DISILLUSIONED

Disillusioned by the lights of the night
Dawn comes speaking truth out loud
You're not a man of innocence
You're not a man that makes much sense
You're not the man of childhood dreams
You're not the man I thought you'd be

Bathed in rapture with the beauty of your soul
Held in torment with the knowledge of the old
Feelings of ambiguities
Makes it hard for one to see
The parody that life presents
To those who no longer repent

Time's irreverence to the mind of those aware
Of life's attempt to disregard the absurd
Moments of tranquility
Tends to set the mind at ease
But still the spectrum of truth sees
Through all of man's abilities

And in the end reality proclaims the blame
Contained within the edifice of one's own flesh
Facts concede to meaningless
Openly they now confess
Important ventures now can rest
To thrive no more or to contest

11

JAN DARROW

GOLDEN BALL

Listen to the music in the stillness
of your heart.
Close your eyes;
see how beautiful you are.

A heavenly choir above me
Sounds an echo in my heart.
A golden ball around me
Keeps me shining like a star.

Live life to the fullest.
Walk through darkness and the light;
Yet keep your heart as pure
As a candle in the night.

All men are brothers.
Joined in love, we are one,
A circle never broken,
Shining brighter than the sun.

SPINNING SONG

I'm spinning 'round the center;
I keep on turning 'round.
So fast I spin, my colors are hid
In a pale gleaming blur.
I won't waste my time in worry
As long as I keep turning.
When my life is done and I am spun,
My Maker will appear.

We are the wool on our Father's wheel.
In a long thread we are spun
For a coat of many colors
To be placed upon His Son.
Oh, my white wool might get dirty,
But I'll wash it once a week,
And I'll put my trust in Jesus,
The spinner of my dreams.

KLAMATH RIVER TRILOGY

SOLITUDE

I watched the full moon rise above
the winding Klamath River
As I sat upon a bluff which
overlooked a triple bend.
There below on steeping slope
a bouncing doe caught my eye,
And I pondered, 'What Paradise,
where no hunter can find her;
Haven for me, a weary human
seeking solitude,
And for her, a gentle deer
seeking food.'
And now the birds come into view;
A gray pair flew, one to a treetop
and one to the water.
All creatures of the night
find safety by the river.
Gentle breeze, and dancing trees,
The crickets raise their song.
As the full moon sheds
her lantern light,
I, too, find shelter
in the night.

KLAMATH RIVER TRILOGY

RIVER DREAMS

Singing along with Kate Wolfe
down the Klamath River Highway,
I head for Dillon Creek
for the full moon in July.
Oh, the winding of the road
and the haunting of her lyric
Cast a spell of sentiment
and freedom of the spirit.
Songs about the love of friends,
and times of joy and laughter,
And songs so sad, your heart
would dump like a Turtle River rafter.
And safe now in my campsite,
I walk down to the swimming hole
And await the rising of the moon
when she lays her veil of gold,
Her pale arm reaching 'cross the water
like a figurine of grace,
To where I sit on a rock alone
with moonlight on my face.

KLAMATH RIVER TRILOGY

RIVER SONG

Moonlight threads a silver needle~
Klamath River at night,
Flowing westward through the canyon,
Weaving gently left and right.
Time unwinds and I feel
like I'm coming home.
Timeless river, speak to me alone.
Thin clouds filter across the sky.
For one sad moment, I heard
a wild goose cry.
Name that tune as the river sings,
Windshield echoes with drops of rain.
Merciful rain in a world of drought,
Preserve these steelhead
and endangered trout.
From what I see,
the highway comes and goes,
But the singing river beside me
ever flows.

THE CARD

When I think I've lost
you forever
A card from you comes in the mail,
And it lays unopened on the table
For I'm afraid to break the spell.
My heart races and I ponder
at the miracle of love,
How in an instant, the thought of
you can renew in me a hope of
Your return, the awakening of Spring,
Making me feel alive again.

TO FLY WITHOUT WINGS

Let go
of roles and reputation
Embrace
The intrinsic beauty
the obvious miracle
of Who You Are

When fear
creeps out
of the shadows
struck blind
in the brilliant face
of recognition
rejoice
as these heavy, brittle logs
of passionate longing
inflame
and stoke the fire
of your burning heart

True Faith is revealed
in the willingness
to doubt
all mistrust
to fly
without wings
plummeting fiercely
through clouds
of illusion
thus soaring
in endless awareness
the limitless flight
of being the sky

SOLITUDE

Dear Solitude
My eternal friend
without you I am alone
rabbled and restless
in confusion I drone

Dear Solitude
Dozing through details
I wake to your soundless call
your whispers beckon
to your company I crawl

Dear Solitude
Mingling in memories
in your breathless embrace
I follow your voice
along streams of laughter I trace

Dear Solitude
I trail the frantic flock
weary, for an instant I pause
and this is where you enter me
my longing united with its cause

A NIGHT IN THE FOREST

Dimming embers glimmer
sparks of crimson-gold
pulsing in surrender
to their fate of ashes
under a canopy
of white-hot coals
of slowly dying suns

The creek murmurs softly
through the hushed night air
while a train shuffles

19

in the valley below
as I rustle into my bag

Resting under starlight
with all the company I desire
the arm of the dipper
draped over my shoulder
and the crisp pine air
skimming my pillow
kissing my breath

One day this body too
capped with curly locks
will simmer into
cinders
just as this glacial peak
of sleeping fire
upon which I rest
will one day blow
and shriek

And on another day
be blown
of its earthly spire
to luminous atoms
by an even greater pyre
of eternal dust

THE CLOCK

The clock has run down.
No longer does it chime.
The pendulum which used to swing
Won't swing at any time.

Its hands that moved so freely,
Have stopped some minutes past.
The hours now unaccounted for
Move their own pace, slow or fast.

Darkness falls and rises bringing us
A new night or a new day.
But no chimes are there to echo out
How long they each will stay.

The old clock stands rigid,
Pressed against the entry wall
It's a silhouette, a timely shadow
Of the clock that stood so tall.

HOPE

Beads of sweat
Caress my brow,
Forming a ring
Of hope in a
Moment of despair.

FRAGILE

You wear your
Emotions
On your sleeve.

Touch you oh
So gently
And you bleed.

You try to mask
Your feelings
To hide the pain.

And yet tears
Keep falling
Like the gentle rain.

Fragile, breakable,
Stamped
Handle with care.

Surround with love
And fragile
No longer is there.

THE FINAL STEP

Four flights up
To a cold wooden bench.
You sit two benches down
Always facing forward.
I have my lawyer,
You have yours.
Fifteen minutes to court,
Yet it is not enough time
For you to be fair.
The time has come and gone
And yet you still barter
For the years spent
Rotting away with you.
Money and a percentage
The only things you know.
The cold wind blows
Through your heart
Until you give
Just a little,
If only I give
More than a lot.
The doors open.
It's judgment day.
Everything I have you
Have already taken away.
I sit before the judge and
Swear I DON'T WANT YOU.
Then it is over.
I've taken the final step.
A step worth taking.
For it is the beginning
Of a series of steps
To a new beginning.
A beginning I thought
I would never see....

SPIDERS

I have never met a spider
I did not hate.
Those long legs dangling
And that web they use for bait.
Yes, spiders aren't creatures
I like to keep around.
They crawl all over ceilings
and walls
And even in showers can be
found.
Spiders are just creepy crawlers
Put here to drive me insane.
That's why when I turn on the
shower,
I just watch them go down the
drain.

THE SILHOUETTE OF TIME

The silhouette of time
Dances across faces of old,
Lingering only to deposit
A wrinkle here or there.
The silhouette of time
Creeps in slowly.
As an artist contemplates
His next stroke of the brush
So ponders the silhouette,
Before depositing its
Ageless outline upon
The canvas of mankind.
I look beyond
The silhouette of time
To dancing eyes
And a sparkling smile.
Reflecting memories of
Youth...a youth not lost
In the silhouette of time.

22

HANDS

Hands reaching out
To grasp
The tattered bus seat.
Hands worn with age
Wrinkled by years spent
In the heat of the sun.
They tell a tale
Of years gone by,
Of years of
Hard work and toil.
A map of fine lines
Leading to the heart
And soul of man.
Worn hands
Painting a picture.
A picture of the past,
Longing for the future.
Hands, reaching out
In the darkness~
Longing for
The support of tomorrow.

CARRY ME AWAY

Carry me away
To an island of my own.
Carry me away
To a place I can call home.

Carry me away.
To a place beside the sea.
Carry me away
To the place I long to be.

As a breeze moves onward
Or waves break upon a shore,
Carry me away,
To a land that I'll adore.

Carry me away
To a warm and peaceful land.
Carry me away,
To a life left unplanned.

FISH AND CHIPS

Fish and chips
Wrapped in newspaper
A hearty dinner for two.
As you dine,
You can read between the lines
Or the pictures just view.

Fish and chips
Wrapped in newspaper
All you add is tea.
I feel sorry for
The bloody fool who
Buys a paper individually.

The time I spent living in Mt. Shasta was the best six months of my life. I loved the snow; the warm, breezy Autumn; the apple grove in back of our little cottage! Oh! And, of course...The Mountain...She was a constant source of spiritual support to me. I have been writing poetry for twelve years, and while living near the mountain I experienced my most prolific writing period. Poetry came through to me in the Mt. Shasta City Park. I loved to sit on a log crossing a small river with a variety of mossy plants and a type of lily pad. One day, my husband and I shall return to our favorite home...for a long visit...hopefully to stay!

THE ART OF LIVING

So Engaged --
 Involvement revolving round
 My enjoyment at being Alive
So Unbound --
 Opened and responsive to all
 That which is of me and Surrounds
So Connected --
 Enlivened! My life conjoined
 With form and content and essence
So Intuned --
 Awakened and aware inside a moment
 My ever-expanding present consciousness
So Quiet --
 Listening to Being's breath rise and fall
 The life of my body a grounding point
So Released --
 Freed, all at once, my Being at One
 With the poetic trance of living!

BALANCE

Who will waken the depths of me
Born to such intensity --
What will charge my Being enough
Surrounding IT, wound about All Such --

Records have themselves traced in me
That I've a million roads of memory --
Visions parade, spontaneous of inner eye
Such that these can create my demise --

In a world overcome by small details
I've inner conflicts no hope can derail --
Yet, this world, such profound power owns
My limitless power matched--studied, practiced, thrown

Past treatise I have drawn now possess
Released in any moment, I am made free --
Blessings descended fulfill this ready vessel
Time drops away where surrender fast-follows.

I & GOD

Life is expanded --
Protected here.
I soak, I swim,
A languid bathe --
In sweet maternal waters.

I am fed dreams --
I proclaimate chemicals
Consume desire --
A thousand times
O'er the night --
And through the day.

This womb provides --
Intriguing life.
I know my unknown --

My ancient wisdom,
My eternal innocence --
Borrowed from past experience.

Reveling in the mysterious --
Inner worlds,
I take my test
And pass --
Extolling time and nothingness.

I breathe creation --
Into fast-forming lungs
Sing of my talents,
Pray them to be actualized --
And consummate my plan
With God!

Along the length --
Of firm-yielding walls
I wait --
My essence becoming earthy
Inside this solitude.
The depths of my self --
And the Woman above
Held so close, so dear
To my innermost heart --
Held here and gently nurtured
By this Woman
None could know
This way --
But I & GOD!

I pray for birth --
Pray for my next becoming,
My reawakening --
Through fluidity of feeling,
Through my development
My graceful learning
Dropping ever-closer to the earth.

Each day this personal evolution --
Pulls upon my senses,
Creating deeper grooves in memory --
As I make my way
From here to my new home --
Amongst humanity.

My soul's journey --
I & GOD
Have between us crafted --
Have decided --
I shall live out my new purpose,
Until once more,
My spirit soars skyward --
          Home to immortality!

CATHERINE GOULD

MY ISLAND

Adventure begins with a fall,
Tower cards, let us say:
A time of loose formation
Within the scape of my mind.

A fall, eternal tower of babble,
Descending in heated frenzy,
Disappears,
Into the easy hum whispering
Of a casuarina tree on a soft white beach.

Now, after the fall, I lie still
Calm ocean sips at my mind
The tide steadily rising, with
The cool intensity of the moon, is
Pulled ever shoreward, to
The inner reaches of my island.

My island, tide rising,
Even the blackness of the night
Cannot pull it back. I am still~
The ocean has swallowed my adventure
And now, all gone, all still,
It is time to move on.

ANGEL DEATH BLOWS ITS TRUMPET TO THOSE WHO WILL HEAR

death,   sitting on the corner
casts an eye to sky
I wonder who is next
thinks death

death,   pulling faces in shop windows
practices looks it cannot feel
sucking on a cigarette
leaves no lipstick traces

death,   waiting in the shadows
of rooms and rumours of fear
I can see it in your eyes
(and my own if I choose)

death,   last meal half digested,
no taste for dessert,
all words and thoughts final
no chance to amend for, or care for, or...

RITUAL IN HA-SHASH-NI-PA

Journeying far, kah thump, kah thump.
Into the wilderness by light by night.
Headlamps off, door open.
Moon is low.

Step onto the hard ground, door close.
Move away from machine and metal
Disappear into the veil
Soft desert sand and night air.

Bitter medicine pulses into my blood
My mind swells, bursts, and breathes once more
I come seeking, I am the seeker
The only answer I expect is the sunrise.

Blanket about my shoulders, I move over the land
The land speaks I listen and laugh
Joys of spirit fill my heart
I am alive, so is the rock beneath me.

Grandmother comes, gift of light upon my mind
Great spirit tells the tales of ancestors, long gone
Ancestors dance, weaving wisdom into my blanket
Moon is high now.

Fire upon horizon, Venus rises dreadfully
She-star pierces, encodes my mind anew
A name, I have now. Initiation over.
The night comes pale.

Dawn draws nearer, fire fades to ash
Leave gift of tobacco, tell coyote-da my name
He'll howl it on the sunrise as I journey far away
Kah thump, Kah thump.

WINDSWEPT WINTER

The way of the windswept winter is here.
She hisses death to all who come near.
The stillness hollow,
Its darkness sorrow,
Emptiness beneath me tomorrow.

INSANE POETS

Poets are insane. It's starting to rain.
Come inside. There's nowhere to hide.

LOVE

Send her your love if you want to keep her;
Live for yourself and your pain will grow deeper.
Love is the way as Paul has said;
Throw it away and you're better off dead.

INTOXICATED MIRTH

We ran and played in the quiet lake,
Drenched in the moonlight...
Of supple, sacred softness,
And we, the fourth couplets, became intoxicated
In the mirth of pleasure; we sat naked
Beneath your sacred star of ecstasy.
We crossed our legs to breathe.
We took in the waters of love
And played there forever. Amen.

THE DEMONS' DAMNATION

They screamed and giggled and laughed
They, the demons as they cheated the man below.
We took his power, he broke his tower
To the last possible hour,
They laughed and sang.
But the man got up...his way was bold...
His stoney fist had turned to hold
The sword of justice and determination.
At last they sank into damnation.

PAIN

I cried...bent and low I sighed.
The pain has shaped a new man.
I'm not the same man I was an hour ago.
No. The way to know
The greatest good of the greatest God
Is pain.
Yes, pain, and not disdain;
Take the pain and never disdain...
Find strength in the pain...it will shape you;
You will never be the same.

LIFE'S PARADOX

　　　　Listen, children, listen to what I have to say.
The chamber of words I have to tell you
Is important all the way.
　　　　The words of wisdom and knowledgeable chance,
It's come to me in a kind of trance.
　　　　For from the Tao it's finally known
That defects are really strengths
Turned upside down.

FIFTY YEARS

Fifty years.
Happy Anniversary, Mother and Father.
A smothered voice,
from the ghost of childhood past.

Children...

Your first one died at birth,
Free from the start.

The second, a nineteen year sentence,
Commuted by death.

Three and four paid the full price.
Life, without parole.

Number five,
Killing her softly with your wrong.

Mother and Father...

Fifty years, a lie.
Time on your hands.
Eyes that shift in the mirror
as they glance away from the truth.

Put away the party hats.
Put away the light.
Crawl against each other
into the coming darkness.

Pull the filthy ones around you.
Hear their whispers,
vile sounds covering the truth
like a shroud.

Fifty years,
incarceration, to be sure.
I'd offer you a seat in hell,

...but you're already there.

"The End"

JANE HOFFMAN

Nineteen years ago our family moved to Mt. Shasta seeking a different quality of life. Like many who dwell on the slopes of Mt. Shasta, I found the beauty and harmony here to be an inner and outer inspiration. Wonderful expressions of the arts abound in this area, and my medium became words. Contemplative poetry began to flow several years ago while my husband and I were on a peaceful vacation in the forest. Poetry is a gift of encouragement to assist me in becoming aware of my thoughts, feelings and words, and take responsibility for what they create.

VACATION

Waking to the first rays of morning, and the diamond dew
My heart in chorus with the birds as they begin to sing
The sweet smell of forest perfume on every breath
The rhythm that awakening with nature brings
Calls me

Sitting in a quiet forest glen, back against a tree
Feeling the strength of these towering friends
Observing their reverence as they bow to every breeze
And non-resistance in their willingness to bend
Calls me

Lying in a hammock, watching distant stars
Listening to the trees whispering in native song
The night breeze dancing with the meadow grass
White glowing embers of a campfire nearly gone
Calls me

And when I spend some time like this, in idleness
I find that hungry place within me filled
And my perspective on important things is changed
Just by listening to that call, to come - be still

35

SNOWFLAKES

Wrapped in warmth of fire's hearth, watching cold December
   sky,
There are swirling gusts of white, hurrying on by.
I gaze upon the window pane, at little flakes of snow,
And ponder in my musing, the simple truth they show.

They arrive as individuals; no two are quite the same,
And they stay until the warmth dissolves them on the pane.
They melt to drops of water, and then by nature's heat,
Are drawn upward in the sky, and their cycle is complete.

But their exquisite crystal presence remains in memory,
For us to ponder on their beauty, and the miracle we see.
They are a glorious creation in their fragile crystal form,
Each a unique pattern, from upper skies they're born.

They don't call for recognition, as they merge in drifts of white
Not one claims to be superior while swirling from their height.
No fight and no resistance, as they land where they are sent,
And express their fleeting beauty, in harmonious content.

CHANGES

What brings two souls together
mortals seldom know,
What is the silent whisper
that calls for one to go?
When lessons are completed
what words are left unsaid,
Where are the many moments
that all too soon have fled?

What memories do we hold
that we would wish to change,
And how many circumstances
should we like to rearrange?
Ah--yes, if we could look ahead
how different we might be,
But it's more often in reflection
that we find our needed key.

Grieve not, when pathways part
for what is lost from view,
Will one day cross again
when the day is ever new.
And each will have the wisdom
gained from lessons learned,
And reap the welcome benefits
that experience has earned.

REACH OUT

How foolish if we, as we walk down the street,
would reach out and kick the ones that we meet.
"Oh sorry my friend, this foot is a knave
it simply does not want to behave."

We restrain our feet, keep our hands in control
as we sit in our seats, or take a short stroll.
But what of our thoughts, as we walk down the street;
do they reach out to strike the ones that we meet?

Do they secretly judge the way others dress
or do they reach out, to love and to bless?
Do your thoughts reach out, to hurt and debase,
Or do you meet others with a heart full of grace?

Do you silently shrink from folks not of your class,
or offer a smile to all as they pass?
Are you repelled by looks, or put off by weight,
or do you see all, as though they were first rate?

Until we control our thoughts as our feet,
and reach out with respect to all that we meet,
We will never be happy, never be whole,
until each errant thought is in love's control.

SOMETIME MAJIK MOMENT

and temples bell of prowling lions
laddered stars guest angels calling
as the mermaids lured with singing
lostlonely ships at sea

dawn and dusk risefell in instants
my fingers trace the spectrumed night
unseen I dare not understand
dreading knowledge more than wisdom

Now is always ever was
taut eternities in notes shining
expiring vibrant through the woods
with surrender uncomprehending

That that only desires to sing
duets with Its creation

ONCE A BUTTERFLY

i was a butterfly once -
soaring on a breath of wind,
turning on my back to see the sun
and bluesky sprinkled with flowered rain.

i was a butterfly once -
showing off
my figure eights
for a ladyfriend.

i was a butterfly
able to lay wings
upon the drifting Peace River
feeling a summerday
fill my soul with truth.

I was a butterfly once -

with you.

RAINCHECK

We are valiant mariners
charting trackless waters
filled with phantasmal fearfulness
while daring to be free

in our storm washed ships we sweep
into God-lit cloudless skies . . .
into a geometry of existence
where fears are juxtaposed with poem

i am the ancient mariner . . . and
you, my bowsprit, are
doweled to my cracked and broken hull . . .
pointing the way to landfall
and the distant stars beyond
someday . . .
someday, when mists are on your sails
and your anchor holds the sands
of some last and lonely port
someday . . .
when that day comes,
call to me in silence
call to me
with our mystic joining song
grant to me the honor . . .

that i may cut the hawser ropes
that have held your spirit fast
within some ancient harbor wall
then . . .
i will come

i will come with tenderness
to lift your shattered being
up . . . up
up into the sunsets we carressed
before you left that lastime

WHEN THE BOUGH BREAKS

A young man dies
Two girls are injured
What is this
An incident or accident
A tree is involved
Along with the alias of a car
People are mourning
And crying themselves to sleep.

The young man
A good one at that
An honest loving young man
Kindness was a must
But happiness?

A never.

For at the age of fourteen
Could it possibly be your time?

Two girls injured
Lightly but feeling other pain,
For the boy in the back
For one young lady,
A slight neck injury
And for the other,
A kidney possibly damaged
But do they care
Yes
But not as much as they mourn
That of a still young man
Lying in the back seat of a car.

Dedicated to Evan Baker: 1980-1995

JEFFREY D. LOUCKS

WRITERS BLOCK?

Charles sat in his room
With his bottle of Rum
He didn't believe in writers block.

He took a shot.

He sat there with his desk
He looked down at the sheet of paper
It was blank
It was not what he wanted to look at
He liked it full
Full of words
No errors to be found
A perfectionist at heart.

He had drunk since four
And written since three
He was greatly published
Yet undermined his public
He thought his stuff was shit
He found it intolerable
And yet he would send it out
No problem
Accepted he would get back
In big bold writing
He was offered contracts
He was given advances
This bewildered him
And now for the first time in his life
He sat there with his Rum
And couldn't come up with a damn thing
Is this the end
He wonders in dread.

He goes to bed
And in the morning
He switches to Brandy.

HERE IS ... (ETC)

Here is the Greatness,

Here is the Greatness,

Here is the Greatness,

Is this true Greatness,

Or is this Greatness,

This is the Greatness,

This, is the Greatness.

In which we lay.

We dwell in each day.

That leaks through our pores.

This manifesto of hope.

A figment of our imagination?

This Horrid Thing We Strive For,

MICHAEL JOHN MCCLURE

Michael was born in Anaheim, California in 1970 and has lived in various parts of the United States. His poetry reflects his fondness for gentle yet powerful truths, and a greater and broader love for Mankind. Michael expresses through the arts and is currently a partner of Singing Tree, a mother-and-son performing duo, whose purpose is to inspire and encourage peace through song, sound, and word.

THE BEAUTY OF THE BROWN

I used to dream that love was Green
and I knew the truth in Blue.
I thought that Red was passion sought
from a lover's point of view.

But there was one whose beauty shone
beyond my wild heart's gaze,
and it was true beyond the Blue,
beyond the Red's hot rays.

But I didn't hear it coming near,
its strange and magnificent sound,
the sound of life beginning deep
in the beauty of the Brown.

In my life I've sought the Gold --
the treasured pure heart's hold,
and Silver gales would guide my sails
to sacred lands untold.

But I could have gone on the path of one
that would have found me home
in the land of Earth and joy's rebirth,
where kinships and friendships warm.

But I didn't see this path of truth,
for concepts held my view.
I only saw a dormant blade of grass
and nothing new.

I felt secure beyond all fear
in the Yellow's blinding light
and Purple's might would lift my sight
to the eagle's soaring height.

But down below where light won't go
there is a world of wonder
where life begins in silent hymns,
then sprouting forth in thunder.

And in this place of life embrace
when light, its touch has found,
you see the glory of its peace
in the beauty of the Brown.

This all is true to all the few
of the colors I have learned
to seek and find, to use in mind,
for the colors I have earned.

And the one that's next
is the one that's mixed
of the Red, the Blue
and the Green;
the one I've missed,
the one I've kissed
yet haven't really seen.

And soon -- very soon
I will have found
The magic in the beauty of the Brown.

45

WEAVE

I am content with life on Ground,
    for, no other life my mind has found.
But, soon my life I will not know,
    for, change is coming;
        the winds must blow.
I think not what lies ahead.
    I find my shelter.
        I find my bed.
I climb the branch to the farthest limb
    and listen to the calming hymn:

        "Weave...
            weave...
                weave..."
    it sings.

        "Weave...
            weave...
                weave..."
    it rings.

I do not know this voice from me
    as I whisper back, "Why should this be?"
"As childhood ends, the child recedes,
    As the path to change, the caterpillar must weave."
A sigh I heave,
    and I start to weave.
        And, as I finish my task, I leave...

...A glimmer of light
   in the darkness around;
A glimmer of thought
   in the stillness;
     a sound.
"Trust in me..."
   It rings.
"Come with me..."
   It sings!
I seem to remember a time long ago,
   this voice of light;
     this voice I know.
"Trust in me,"
   says the starless night.
"Come to me, my gentle delight."
This voice, it beckons and calls to my heart
   I reach
     and I stretch
     and long to be part
of this glorious melody from somewhere beyond
   the boundaries of Earth.
   I need to respond.
   "Take me to where my heart can be free
     to soar with the breeze.
   Creator, change me."

"With greatest of love I'll change you to be
   another joy to the world
and reflection of me.
Rest in my palm and surrender your view."
   And as I laid in Love's hand
   I became something new.

I was content with life on Ground,
     for, no other life my mind had found.
   But, then my life, I did not know,
     'till change occurred
And now I glow.

FORGIVENESS

Blame harms the one who thinks it,
speaks it.
Guilt harms the one who feels it,
weeps it.
Forgiveness is the one who cleans it,
sweeps it,
and loves it...
all...
away...

SALLY J. MCKIRGAN

Sally is an artist, poet and environmentalist, born on the Olympic Peninsula, Washington state, former resident of San Francisco and now dividing time between Oregon and California. She believes an artist's job is to awaken minds and help heal wounded hearts.

THE HOXIE-GRIFFIN STAND

Once upon nineteen ninety six in the State of Oregon
There was some tall timber that was wanted by some
A great stand of trees called the Hoxie-Griffin sale
Come let me tell you about this tree cutting tale.

In timber land it's called a "stand," a universe of trees
Their beauty overcoming, a wilderness to please
Two hundred fifty acres on the Pacific Crest Trail
If this lonely stand should fall, all Creation would wail.

But the Salvage Rider Law was made to take big trees
The President and Congress for the lumbermen to please
The People who protect the trees came to their side
Wanting only to help nature quietly abide.

They found the trees cut and wounded in the deep pure snow
Crying out softly saying they just wanted to grow
Some put their bodies between the trees and machines
Trees yet to fall calling "Help" shining through the green.

Next time you hike along the Pacific Crest Trail
Walk through the woods to see why thirty went to jail
The smell of pitch, the scent of fir lingers on the mind
A sustainable way of life is feasible to find!

49

Now rains have flooded rivers and salmon eggs have drowned
And clear cut ravaged hillsides have all come tumbling down
Causing millions in damage to the Pacific Northwest
Ancient forests are gone and loggers think they know best.

Oh loggers please choose again, a way of life must change
Let us help each other so a family we'll remain
Come along oh fathers, mothers, sisters and sons
We only need remember that we all are One.

FRANCIS W. MANGELS · BARD FRANCIS GOODFELLOW

I came to Mt. Shasta from Montana in 1981 to work as a
biologist. The area's natural history and special places became a
focus I love to share with friends. I hope you will join us to
exercise your creativity for a better world.

AQUILIAN SONG

If wings were sonnets, what a message they would bring!
If they were both, then surely they would be a song.
If three, then surely could this creature rise to sing,
On pinions slender, sure, so swift and strong.
Such wondrous ways to wander heaven's world,
Where wind the winds of whispy clouds unfurled.
At ease with every strand those avian eyes,
And asking each until the quest espies
A beauteous beating breast beside his own,
Which flies where few in flowing song have flown.
Then soon their talons clasp to joy's rebirth,
And crying to their souls, they fall toward earth.

EAGLE SONNET

So shall they seek the sun with shining souls,
Soon soar the shifting swirls of rising air.
Wing to wing away with wondrous goal,
By power, by grace they find the fastness fair.
Anon, have other of adventure raised,
Sought so to send such spirit sooth to flight.
Some swifter, some sincerely so are praised.
Aquilians alone attain all height.
So shall they sing, who dare the dome of sky,
And rainbows herald high here heavens flown.
How few may hark and hear the high-thrown cry,
Exultant up above the earth alone.
In heaven's halls, mist-masters of the air,
While we below rejoice to see them there.

COFFEE CANTATA

I have seen the living coffee bean tree and lived to tell the tale.
Known the depths of passion spun fine from a coffee grinder.
Reason left on the doorstep
I venture through virgin territory--the dark night of the soul.
Cross of cherry bark, Sumatra in my veins, I stumble down
pathways of EXISTENCE. Aroma of coconut cream weakens my
will. I surrender to the armies of coffee traders.
Thieves who ply their trade upon meek maidens and turn them
into helpless fools. I live from cup to cup.
A cup, a cup, a cup...

CONFESSIONS OF A COFFEE MANIAC

Tonight, I dream of Jamaican Blue Mountain.
No ordinary Kona blend will do. Tell Juan Valdez to get lost or
sell it to the Columbian Cartel. I crave the best brew of the
house. Dark Arabica beans bursting with flavor and just a hint
of surprise. Oh, see it in my eyes, I'm addicted to this Java Jive.
Au Chocolat, of Thee I sing.
"They call me coffee, 'cause I grind so fine."

(This last line comes from a poem by my friend, Willie Sims)

THE POET

The poet wants to go to EXCESS
The ascetic wants to even out the highs and the lows.
Caught in the crossfire
I discover I'm not a Bodhisattva yet;
Just a mortal wounded
On the battlefield of life.

APRIL FLOWERS

Kiss the April flowers
See the morning dawn
Dew-dappled diamonds
Upon the grassy lawn
Heaven is within us
Hear the angels cry
Kiss the April flowers
Hear the fairies sigh
While the heavy dew drips
Down among the April flowers.

COME TO POETRY

Come to Poetry
Poetry is better than sleep!
Frankincense for the tongue
My soul to keep.
The caravan moves on across the desert sands.
The world is large & dreams are vast.
We shall find love, truth and fame
Enough to fan the flame.
Oh hunger for milk & honey
I sing a bedouin refrain
There is no God but God
& Poetry is her name!

THE POINT OF IT ALL

What has my life been, what am I here for,
Why all the pain and strain, and now and then gain,
Was there a lesson to learn, the good and the bad,
Was there a goal to seek, my destiny planned,

Why all the heartache, the plans that went wrong,
Were these frustrations, to make me more strong,
Why all those dreams inspiring, those fantasies exciting,
That couldn't be reached, but were so inviting.

So here's to the future, goodbye to the past,
Here's to my life, seeking love that will last,
So here's the last chapter, I'll answer my call,
Fulfilling my quest, as destiny calls,

I'll live loving life, as though forever lasting,
I'll find a true love that grows everlasting,
Here's to the future, I'll never look back.
At last I have learned the point of it all.

OF PENNIES AND OTHER THINGS

a pocket full of pennies
makes up this thing,
my life...full of changes
and other things...

in days of old
when bells were sold,
my heart did ring
as my spirit lay cold...

a pocket full of nickels
is what this one owed,
with one lonely pocket
on one broken load...

in days of new
the nickels they flew,
up into dreams
seen within my means...

a pocket full of change
to be held, felt and seen,
is what we are left with
in this in-between...

in days of now
I wonder how
all the jumps, leaps and crawls
brought me through these halls...

a pocket full of pennies
sure makes up this thing,
my life...full of changes
and desiring to sing...
of pennies and other things...

BETTA NEAL

DRESS CODE

My entire life is a fashion statement
I go on doing what I do
Different from everyone else
Misunderstood
Resented
And only because they're too afraid to know me
They hate me because they can't control me
My unpredictability has driven me towards madness
There is no place for me
I don't belong
I can't be normal because then I'd be like them
All that's left is who I am

JUST A SMALL THOUGHT

The world is full of real land,
real water, real plants,
real animals, real stars in a real sky
and fake people walking the real
Earth

NOT UNTITLED

Erratic misery
Peaceful racket
Dreams of order
Thoughts of calm
Life of chaos
NOWHERE'S home

A NOTE FOR ME

A baker's dozen ravens stand
My poem, my way
Only I can say
A line I can't think of writing
All existence
Is it nonsense?
Stare into an empty coffee cup
How confusing I seem
I start to daydream
I see a gawky stare in the mirror
My inner child reborn
All roses have thorns
I sit and write a note for me
Remember my next first kiss
And my note read like this...
Hi.

SENSIBLE NONSENSE

My strange ways
are accountable
from many days
of agony and denial
that the mistakes made
were mine and no one
else's

WHAT A MOON

Blue moons are white
New moons aren't there
I can never find the other
half
And a quarter moon buys
more than a penny
You can tell when it's
empty
And the man in the moon
never smiles or frowns

THE CUP

The cup isn't half full
And it isn't half empty
Look from both sides
The water line is in the
middle

57

LAZYCAT

Lazycat
Without a care
How I wish
That I was there
Basking
In the sun all day
Catching mice
Is your delay
Lazycat
Without a care
How I wish
That I was there

THE DREAM WORLD

The dream world
You want to live in
Away from the reality
Beautiful dream
Wonderful miracles
Why do we have to leave
Such a wonderful place
But here I am
In the real world
Dark cold floating
In the image of man

GREED

Greed creates war
Love breaks hearts
Fear makes us weak
Hate makes us cold
And friends make us strong

A SHADOWY WORD

A shadowy word --
What is it?
(I ask myself)
(And I reply)
A word --
Not meant to be heard
Or a word --
Not meant
To be spoken
Maybe a thought
Or just a feeling
What is a shadowy word?

A FAR AWAY MEMORY

A far away memory
A far away thought
Lost in time
I can't make it out
But I remember it
So clearly
Just like it was
Yesterday
Or was it
A million years ago
Maybe it was real
Maybe it wasn't
How can you tell?

LINDA NEAL

INSPIRATION

What was that thought I had
Without device to cordon off
Our best dreams
Are likely to escape
Flutter in our waking
Take wing and sing aloft
True art stems from these
Fleeting electrons
Gathering round the moon
In bands of rainbow hue
And me and you
Trying to share
Some piece of the sky

AMBITION

I wanted to be the kind of mother
To share with you the wonders of the world
In every stone you pick up
Each bundle of flowers that you gather
From the jungle of our yard
Stretched out in the prickly lawn
Picking out the shapes that sail across the sky
Horses, pups, iridescent dancing dragon flocks
That circle the crags and come to light on the mountain
I wanted to be the kind of mother
Who values all you are or want to be
Discovering along with you the mysteries of life
Echoes of the universe you bring to the surface of my soul
To give you all you need even room to grow
To help you guide your course and open wide your mind
I wanted to be...and I am...and here I am
Nagging you to do the dishes

THROW YOUR SORROW TO THE WIND

Live a meditation
Love a life away
Don't wait until tomorrow
Be happy for today
Life is but a season
A twinkle in God's eye
Take joy in no good reason
To laugh as time goes by
Your life begins each moment
You sing and dance and play
So throw your sorrow to the wind
And love your life away

GOAL SETTING

Where is my life?
   Where my life is going
      Living Russian Roulette
         I think I know
            And set my course
               To be found at 180 degrees
                  Right angles control my destiny
                     Oh I try and won't give up
                        The delusion I might have the choice
                           To do just that myself
                              Pending floods and toxic wastes
                                 Political hopscotch that goes on
                                    Above my head and below my feet
                                       And with no consent of mine

61

ODE TO THE AIRCRAFT MECHANIC

All night long the planes appear,
From New York, L.A. and everywhere.

The passengers come, the passengers go,
What makes 'em fly they don't know.

Cockpit door opens, flight crew appear,
Captain, first officer and flight engineer.

They fly the plane, yes that is true,
Haven't you ever wondered what the mechanics do?

They check the plane from nose to tail,
Check all the systems so they won't fail.

They sign their name that all's okay,
That she'll fly safely through another day.

Now, you may have been told (amongst other things)
That a plane flies on its engines and wings.

Yes, thrust and lift may bear her flight,
But it takes a good "mech" to keep her all right.

So, next time you fly and give thanks to the crew,
Remember the "mechs" and all that they do.

MEDITATION

What's meditation, ask me not,
For I'm just a fool writing what I see.
Ask the flower who is to me,
In perfect love through God's beauty.

Or the tree whose meditation is,
Only rustled by the breath of the wind,
In her hours of stillness,
Or the trembling of the earth.

The spider spinning her web,
Is construction for a greater purpose.
Not to catch her prey,
But to allow the time
To meditate and observe
The blossoming of all life.
From her silken prow,
She sees all life,
And yet somehow
I feel she opens not her own eyes.

Who said what's big is great,
And what's small is small?
Who's to say that a spider
Is not the king of us all?

A WRITER

Who said I'm a writer; was it a friend?
A writer, a writer; oh what an end.
You're sensitive and you feel the pain,
You have to write to keep yourself sane.
They say the words flow from the heart,
Suffer some pain, that's when they start.
But, when the words come to an end,
The pain's still there and,
Where's your old friend?

MOVIN' ON

I see the light of the holy one,
See my old life; it's movin' on.
My teachers appear, day by day,
Leading me along on my way.

I turn my head, say good bye,
Extend my hand. Begin to fly.
I break the bonds of the material plane,
Sometimes I wonder if I am sane.

I see things, things I can't say,
Things of God, things while I pray.
I begin to talk, but I don't speak.
The words are God, strictly unique.

Words of strength, strength I can feel;
Words of faith, faith that can heal.

My physical needs are the needs of one,
I understand the work that has to be done.
Physically I have become a light,
One that can be seen by the physical sight.

The beams all shine to infinity,
So all can see, all can be.
Take my hand, touch the sky.
With the knowledge of God, we all can fly.

MY KINGDOM

My kingdom of one, one that is all,
No door, no bridge, no moat, no wall.
The trumpets sing, sing out with might,
For all to come, come to the light.

Not all look up, not all can hear
The beautiful sounds blocked by their fear.
They say they have the faith in God --
Why then the fear; isn't it odd?
So, place your life in the hand of Him,
And the light you seek may never be dim.

STEPHANIE SAMPLE

I was born Stephanie Sample in San Jose, CA. When I came into this world I thought it was as loving, kind, warm and fair as my mother's smile; I was wrong. So I write, with the passion that consumes me, of the struggles between both worlds. The two poems I chose are my view of the world today and my feelings for a friend who has left this mortal life but while here blessed many with the beauty of friendship.

CRYING OUT

Where is the humanity
Where's it all gone
I am suffocating in this world
I cannot breathe
With so much greed, who can survive
We aren't living, just existing
I want peace for all people
But people want turmoil
I want families to love one another
Without judgment or expectations
This world is upside down
Are all our souls dead inside
Have our spirits all been crushed
Do we not have an ounce of compassion
Am I all alone in what I believe
Do you hear the cries of the forgotten
Will I become cold and bitter
For I would surely rather die
God, please help us find our way
Please help us to follow your way.

FOR BILL

I looked for you in a dream the other night
It was a beautiful, clear blue day and I took to flight
I pushed off, opened my arms as wide as I could
I was flying
I could feel the wind on my face
And the glow of the sun
I searched for you in the hills and valleys
That were all around
I could not find you
Soon the sky became dark and cloudy
I was getting cold and frightened
"Where is my friend," I cried inside
I must protect him from the storm
I was flying fast towards the ground
Feeling out of control and very confused
Before I hit the ground I awoke
And you were with me
You are in my heart and in my memories
I looked to the sky and felt a calmness
You were here all the time
You may be free from this world on earth
But you will stay alive forever in my thoughts
I will miss you my friend
You touched my heart
I love you

A DAUGHTER'S PRAYER

Dear God up above, over the land I live,
please cleanse me and shower me
through love that you give.
I've called on you before, Lord,
but not like I am now.
Please give me the courage
and your strength to know how
to forgive Mom and Dad for all the pain that I feel.
They just left me as a child...
Dear Lord, help me heal.
Dear God, please explain why this happened to me?
You must have a reason for letting this be.
When I am at rest, and put in a grave,
could you answer my questions?
By then I'll be brave.

SISTERS

Have you ever asked yourself the meaning
about what sisters are?
It's a bond we share that can't fall apart
even when you are so far.

So many years have passed us by
and yet our paths still meet.
Although our lives are not the same,
we share a love that can't be beat.

Next time you find yourself alone
and need your sister's touch,
just read these words that I wrote down;
I love you very much.

There's not a day or night goes by
that I don't think of you
because of special thoughts I have
in everything we do.

I'M IN CONTROL NOW

From a child to a grown-up
there's confusion from the past,
feeling pain and sometimes anger...
these emotions must not last

If I go on remembering
what really hurt before,
this could only put a limit on
my future's naked door

The time has come to live or die,
and yes, I did decide
to let go of my childhood
and live a life with pride

Though memories that used to hurt
had hidden me away
until I found the strength to fight,
made peace for yesterday

Each day I know those memories can't hurt
'cause I've moved on
the freedom I have taken back is mine,
from dusk to dawn

GOODBYE MOM

The time has come to say goodbye and lay to rest my past
But it's real hard to let you go when you gave up so fast.
You brought me in the world to live; I thought to be your baby,
But as you know away we went to live with a strange lady.

To get us back you knew the rules; you had to stop the drugs;
As before you sent us off, with kisses and small hugs.
You should've stopped the life you chose, to prove your love
was real;
Instead our pain continued on. You gave no time to heal.

69

As years went on I thought for sure, your children you would
      miss.
You promised we would all come home as you gave us one last
      kiss.
Can you see why it is so hard to say goodbye to you?
We never had a chance to live like families often do.

Mom, all you ever had to do was prove that we belong.
But you gave up and passed away, as we wonder what went
      wrong?

INVADED

Won't you tell me what went wrong
And why the world I knew is gone

I played with Barbies yesterday
And now they just get in my way

I used to think my life was fine
Until a man took what was mine

Years have gone and now I know
A child's innocence will never go

I know it's hard to understand
How pain came from a trusting hand

I met that monster, just like you
You must believe; what could we do?

MOMMA'S GARDEN
(Co-written with my brother, Eddie Schuyler)

Mom's heart was like a garden, old fashioned,
quaint and sweet
At once her life had blossomed
with death came God's retreat
In fields sweet violets hide away
unseen as we pass by
While lilies pure as angels' thoughts
on earth we all must die

Forget me not dear Mother
for perfection I have sought
As the purple pansies blossom
followed by a tender thought
The flowers that have blossomed
began on sacred ground
Like perfume, the scents exquisite
we enjoy this all year 'round

And in Mom's quiet garden
holds the secrets in her heart
Song birds always sing there,
God's creations where we start
Although a rose has beauty,
its thorns cut like a knife
sweet as the breath of roses
blows the fragrance of her life

MOM, ARE YOU THERE?

My nights turned to gray and cold,
I need my mother here to hold
When I think about you, I begin to cry
And you're not around to wipe my eye
Hold me, Mom, hold me awhile
I need to feel your warming smile

SHIRLEY SCHUYLER

Someday soon we'll both embrace,
The pain will be gone, with only a trace
Remember the day when life was a toy
To you in your heart, I was your pride and joy
Then heroin became a big part in your life
37 stitches in your throat from a knife

Your looks became hard, your smile decreased
I realized then, drugs can't be released
You never told me just how you felt
Abuse began then, when you brought out the belt
I'm going away now in a fairytale sleep
I'm sorry, Mamma, I'm beginning to weep

I PLUMB FORGOT

I walked into a cold, worn house, the curtains drawn with fear.
I never knew a house could feel so strange; it's almost queer.
The boogie man came in my home just to frighten me.
That boogie man is really here, my gosh, who could it be?
I stepped onto a blue carpet ground;
Slowly I started looking around.
I advanced my step towards the hall.
I quickly leaned against the wall.
I thought to myself, I'll give it a try...
Apples, peaches, pumpkin pie.
As I looked straight ahead with a terrifying glare,
That light in the living room, I wonder who's there?
I started running and screaming, and shouting real loud,
Just to find out my brother was dressed in a shroud.
I had plumb forgot it was Halloween Night.
When I woke up, tucked so neatly and tight,
Mommy and Daddy leaning over me
 Asking softly, do you want some candy?

ADAM SELIGMAN

Adam Ward Seligman is the author of the critically acclaimed novel *Echolalia* (Hope Press), and an anthology of first-person stories about Tourette Syndrome, *Don't Think About Monkeys*. His most recent book is *The Marriage Vow*, a volume of love poetry and essays written with his wife, poet Julie Ann Furger. Poems in *The Marriage Vow* were first shared with others through the public poetry readings of THE WELL VERSED.

LOST IN THE DREAM

I'm lost in the dream,
Lost in the whale-dream,
Host to vagrant dolphin thoughts,
Of seas past.

I'm lost in the whale-dream,
Adrift in the tides,
Piping air through my snout,
Breathing in the sea.

I eat fish breathe water sing, laugh and love.
I am lost in the whale-dream from the water above.

I'm lost in the dream,
Lost in the man-dream,
The ships of metal racing past
As they sing to me.

I'm lost in the dream,
The quest for inner water peace,
For outer water light,
For the love of a porpoise fair.

I'm lost...so lost,
I sink down to the bottom where
The kelpies grow, where the sand below
Rises up the algae above.
I rise I rise and float up to the surface,

Break water and flex my beak, whistle
And hear her voice in the sky trilling back to me.

Caught in the whale-dream are we all.
Lost. So lost at sea.

THE SACRED GROVE

You will never know me as I know myself,
And I will never know you true.
We can meet in the *Sacred Grove,*
Where once only lived Goddesses and their priestesses.

But what of us? You ask. A whisper heard in the
Night air, that touched at my heart strings
And brought me down to the drinking pool
Where you wash your hair and soothe your aches.

Of us? I answer.
Well, there's work, sacred poetry,
That will earn us a night or two in heaven.

There's family, our future children, our now-living pets.
They will (and do) bring us solace
As the night turns cold
And the snow falls sweetly to Earth.

There is our love, our secret enigmatic Tourettic love.
The cold ground below, the hot sun above.

I can't truly know you or you know me
Until we meet in the *Sacred Grove,*
Strip ourselves of our pretensions and make love
Like little monkeys by the Castle Crags Road.

And then, maybe *only* then,
We will know something of each other,
Out of the sweat, the warmth and the inner glow
Of our *Sacred Love.*

THE CIRCLE

We are standing in a circle, you and I.
You speak, I hit, *we* die.
It is our way, our family's way.
It ends tonight -- it ends today.

"No more," you cry.
"No more," I sigh.
Pattern of abuse and ill-use
Reaches up towards the sky.

We are lying in a circle, you and I.
You speak, I laugh, *we* fly.
It is our way, *our* way.
It starts tonight -- it starts today.

LIFE FORM (An excerpt from a work in five parts)

The light shines out of the tree-tops and illuminates the African
plain,
The lion roars as the helicopter floats overhead and the darts
are fired,
By biologists intent on their prey.
The lioness watches her mate fly overhead and she cries
In pain and in solitary grief.
Her mate is gone.
And where is *God?*
In the beleaguered city in Bosnia empty-stomached children
starve
While fat soldiers rape their mothers and deny criminal
activity,
Because, after all, this is war--this is a holy cleansing ordered
from above.
Yet war isn't so clean after all,
And one soldier resists and is shot dead.
And where is *God?*
When, oh when, will *God* come?

MADDALENA SERRA

Maddalena lives in Mt. Shasta, but grew up in Sardinia, an island in the Mediterranean. She admits that living in the Mt. Shasta area can be attributed to fate, not a free choice. She now owns and runs an Italian restaurant in Dusnmuir. Maddalena misses the ocean but finds the mountains very inspirational. She was born an artist; though a commercial artist by trade, she now cooks, paints and writes -- all artistic expression taking different forms. Her introspective poetry explores emotions and feelings. Maddalena wishes she had more time to write.

ZAMORA

Round curves in shades of gold.
Soft clouds.
Rolling mounds
like swelling walls of flowers.
Melting shades of amber
deep in the shadows
of the summer.

PAIN

Like rain
    it pours
Like thunder
    it roars
Like heat
    it scalds
Like water
    it flows
Like fire
    it burns
And when it passes,
it leaves only ashes.

WHAT

What I see when I look in your eyes
is the glaze of hidden tears
What I hear when I look at your mouth
is the scorn of your ideas
What I feel when I look at your hands
is the work of many years
What I sense when I look in your heart
is your fears.

WONDERER

From sea to shore,
shore to sea,
we wonder in and out of our lives.
We travel the routes of the ancient mariners,
we sail our lives,
modern wonderers,
for new beginning
and no ends.

ISLAND GIRL

I am an island girl,
deep as the sea
blue as the sky
soft as the sand
free as the wind
dark as obsidian
hot as the sun.
I am an island girl.

WATERFALLS

Golden waterfalls
cascading in pools of fresh water
like blue pearls of mutant shades.
I find my reflection
in the deep pools of your eyes.

B.P. STEWART

PASS HERE WITH ME

Pass here with me, beyond all desires,
Beyond the suffering from within;
That mental bondage of the heart.
Light a candle on the window shelf,
I watch as the light of its flame dances
With the fickle breeze.

And right before me, with the light of this candle
The love of all the world shines if I wish...
And it is a true metaphor that the candle is Christ-like
And that we are all made of the same tallow.

Outside the hills are golden in wild grains of oats
And timothy grass. An image of a youthful daydream now
Long passed, I fly now and paint the seas blue.
My eyes watch the sun pulling the moon across the sky.

Oh look, in the wing of a bird you can see the eye of God
As it flies through the sunbeam. And in the water of the bay
Below I'll paint a salmon flash while I listen to the cobbles
Roll under foot of a fisherman way up stream where
The river is far from losing itself through the delta.
I see now. I hear, yes, God paints as we wish to do,
The sky across the ocean, one sea so blue.

And so, the monks ask only their shadows,
Oh was it Tao or Zen?
Who once began to think of life as a stream.
Or John the Baptist before there were Trappists
Who would make my soul so clean.

I was blind for such a long time that the reaper
Made his catch. Then Mary spoke the voice of hope
As she handed me the match.
Light the candle on the window sill
And dance with the fickle breeze.

SHIVA'S WRATH

You cannot enchant me,
You see I am already free.

For now I see the folly in which you cast --
Yes, like a spell, but I won't dance.

So I bring my snake magic from my bag,
My bite poisonous and deadly, I'll watch as you gag.

This is a warning and heed my call,
You have played with an old one and now you'll fall.

Faraway, faraway I dare you to fly,
For now the trance is I.

You in the field, playing ignorant like a child,
Your macho egotism, your phallus wild.

It is not one pitted against each other,
It is about one calling destruction upon another.

Fool's words, parting ways,
You cannot escape the old one's gaze.

THE SOUND OF THE WIND

The wind ran through my hair
The eagle screamed off my back
The fish swam away
And my brother black bear took strikes at the fish
My sister falcon swooshed over my head
My old brother the horse ran on the grass of the green field
My old sister the deer scattered across the forest
The sound of the wind.

I've been writing poetry, stories, novels, plays since I was eight years old. My work has appeared in the *Wisconsin Review, Artwell, Unity Magazine,* and the *Sacramento Bee* where I was a columnist; my latest play was performed in Shasta County in 1994. I'm presently working on my PhD in literature and creative writing and am an English teacher at COS. I love living in and writing about Siskiyou County!

CAT LAP TIME

Purring warmth into my lap, my cream cat curls
into her thick November ball. I blend into her,
stretching, then relax into the ebony shelf
holding the Christmas Cactus.
Five flowerless years I watered
it, praying, waiting, forgetting.
This year it blooms, each green stem drips
a bud
or a gentle five-pointed bloom.
Rich red buds snuggle into the room's grey lap,
into my late night evening surrendered
to the breath of loved ones,
to the curl of their lives
about my bones.

AT THE BASE OF MOSSBRAE FALLS
DUNSMUIR, CALIFORNIA

Seeking the solace of wet granite, I follow the Dunsmuir
railroad tracks through black oak canyon walls dotted with shy
poppies.
Inhaling the raw musk of diesel oil, cedar sap, scotch broom,
last night's showers,
I slide down huckleberry slopes
to the snow-swollen banks of the Sacramento River,
tumble into tightly curled maidenhair ferns
at the waterfall's base, then nestle into its slate ledge,
draping myself with white iris, dense green moss, sweet peas.
Blood red roots of cedar, sycamore embrace me. From its nest,
the black phoebe calls to me. I am home, again,
at last.

BIRTH MARKS

Though named Sycamore Avenue, the lane was lined
with ancient Dutch Elm trees whose thick trunks
could easily have housed the seven dwarves. I, Snow White
at autumn, danced a fall carnival, pirouetting into enormous
sweet sapped piles of yellowed leaves. At the tip of twilight,
I dipped deep into the leaves' belly, inhaling
the sweet musk of those freshly falling,
burrowed to the near night womb of crackling brown leaves,
gnarled roots, bare skinned branches,
suckled at the breasts of ghouls, madwomen, queens.

STEVE TORREY

A local Mount Shasta resident who has been writing poetry since the early 1970's, Steve Torrey's writing covers an array of subjects from contemporary to cowboy and civil war era poetry. Steve has done numerous theatrical as well as public and private recitings, and has also aired on public radio and television. He has been certified an official bard by The Band of Bards writing group of Redding, CA. in addition to his membership in THE WELL VERSED.

JIGSAW PUZZLE

A jigsaw puzzle lay scattered in pieces,
the beautiful tranquil scene all jumbled and mixed
into little bits now a broken shattered dream.
Confusion in battalions, a thousand pieces on the floor
in a perfect state of disarray;
what image will these pieces form?

For each one has its perfect place.
That spot no other one can fill,
as the puzzle master sorts them out.
A piece of sky or a distant hill.
He sees the larger picture as he plays with bits of imagery,
part of a leaf, a piece of twig;
then bit by bit a beautiful tree.
As that pile of mass confusion
now surrenders to his hand,
a beautiful tranquil picture begins to form again.

I stop and ponder deep within
as piece by piece I understand.
Sometimes my life is a jigsaw puzzle
that needs the puzzle master's hand.

STEVE TORREY

WINTER NIGHT

Wind swept the moon,
Slips in the dark of night.
Is it the light that brightens so,
Or just the snow so very white?

The shapes of pointed silhouettes
Rise frigid to the stars.
It's cold I know, so very cold,
But oh how beautiful they are.

Ten thousand trees all point their way
To heaven's endless heights,
While frozen blues and blacks and grays
Compete to paint this winter night.

SIMPLE COMFORT

Strange streets, strange town, nothing looks the same.
From the place where I was yesterday, everything has changed.
No familiar people, just strangers passing by.
Surrounded yet so lonely, like a star out in the sky.
A man walks by, he peers at me through dull streaked steamy
glass.
Then quickly turns his head away, as I sit staring back.
A cop car sits across the street, its grey chrome bumpers glare.
The prisoner waiting in the back sits silently and stares.
And in the distance cold dark hills lay smothered by grey
clouds,
create the perfect ambience for the strangeness of this town.
And the only comforts I can find in this town without a friend,
is this steaming cup of coffee and the movement of my pen.

TREESINGER

Treesinger is part American Indian and lives in Mt. Shasta. This person can be contacted through THE WELL VERSED if you are interested in Treesinger poetry.

NIGHT CALL

Who? Who-Who? Who?
A voice is calling to itself
Somewhere in Panther Canyon.
The Ancient Forest still stands there,
Standing still despite the heretic hands,
Fingers of dirt scratching further
Up this holy Shasta mountainside,
Climbing this Altar of Ages.

The voice watches, silent by day,
Seeking answers in the forest of the night.
Who will answer?
By day the fingers reach, clutching tree by tree,
Climbing the mountain to the canyon,
Higher by day, to rest at night.
When the voice calls, Who will answer?

Who Who-Who? Who?
The prayer arises in the cathedral of Ancients,
Sacred columns too old to be forgotten
By the fingers of the heretic hand,
Or the supplicant's prayer in the night.
Who will answer?

The Inquisitor's aisle of contention
Now lies frozen in the winter of our choice.
The voice has departed to warmer lands.
Next year they meet upon the Altar of Ages.
We will answer in sacrilege and sacrifice.

85

LILY VALLEREY

Writing under a pen name, Lily was born Marlene Lois Gebhart in Dayton, Ohio, grew up in Southern California, lived in Texas during the sixties, and traveled the U.S. extensively before settling at Mount Shasta in 1975. She's been employed with Mercy Medical Center Mt. Shasta for 16 years; however, Lily considers writing her true vocation. From her two marriages, parenting of two sons, an array of rich intellectual, spiritual and experiential settings, and the initiatory power of Mount Shasta, the crucible of Lily's creative writing grew. Writing of poetry began in 1970. The novel started in 1977, *From Seed to Shining Seed,* is now complete, and groundwork for the second novel has begun under the working title -- *The Formless Path: Into the New Millenium.* For this writer..."Poetry has insinuated itself as a bridge to weave vision into rhythm, a quest to name the unnamable, a transcendence of our feeling of isolation. The poetic art affords glimpses through those momentary windows into inner expression. There is boundless joy in the writing and the singing of the song, and the expression of evolution through words." The poetic guild called THE WELL VERSED and their anthology emerged from the seed of her thought.

THE WATERCOLOR TERRACE
for derrick

sunbathed brick walls
and stone foot paths
transformed the unease
of my first visit...

distant sea sounds
calmed my anxious quandary
crimson courtyard roses
carpeted with petals
the path to your door...

86

you opened readily
to my few taps
the splendid grace
of your eyes
validated all the miles

a grim address to go in search of
i feared to find you hungry
in desperate dirt and doubt
what relief the watercolor terrace

it took all day
to drive the caramel highway
no way to let you know
no way to know you'd be there

light, shadow, spare words
avowed your rite of passage
allowed my passage too
through motherhood to friend

LILY VALLEREY

SILENT SONG

the ticks of the clock fall irregularly;
they make the quiet a tangible thing
'til silence fills the room like smoke.
i am Here and Now; and there is nothing else.

thoughts were little creatures running through my head
'til i became a grateful prisoner of silence.
the still chased them away with the day,
so i'm left here alone in the nighttime of my mind.

quiet stillness soothed my body
until i forgot it and left it behind
as my thoughts ascended from the world of words,
ineffably to find the world of knowledge.

whirling memories seek out a red and green key
to the things i know somewhere in the middle of me...
perhaps it's in my heart...
and suddenly the spinning ends.

when peace flows over me in silent softness,
i'm melting slowly into the Forever-Life i've been...
and neither time nor space can remove me from this place.
neither youth nor age can touch the things i know.

i am a self-taught man...for the knowledge was always there,
but fear stood guard against my immortality,
the rage of living bound my head up in despair.
so now the roots of love are strong and alive.

and from the roots of love grows the flower of my youth,
the ageless seeking mind growing toward the light of life
and bringing to my eyes an everlasting fire
shining from the hiding place of my curiosity and desire.

THE SUPREME PATH OF CONTINUOUS PRESENCE

they see dread 'round every corner
they say we've gone to hell in a handbasket
they say you can't trust your best friend
they say all hope is lost

i see us shining in splendor
i say we're linked in dynamic friendship
i say we're embracing change and transformation
i say everyone's being renewed

he asked did she read the front page
she asked if he saw that news flash
he said everybody's dyin'
she said we're destroying our planet

we asked if they read higher teachings
we asked if they saw the Clear Light
we said everybody's livin'
we said our real condition's perfect

let's sing the Songs of Rising
let's walk our paths together
let's serve the cause of knowing
let's touch our cosmic sources

then knowing our true nature
then seeing liberation
then striving for perfection
then finding splendid wisdom

we'll be in the present moment
we'll be ready for transition
we'll maintain continuous presence
we'll join the Light of the One

WINTER MOMENT

barren trees
are cracks in soft gray skies;
mist dripping from their branches,
the sky is shattered...leaking.

shivering,
sat huddled at the window,
the tracery of trees
plays in my memories.

my eye sees
nature's golden child
in sunspots on the ground,
in brightness all around.

whispering,
your softness speaks to me,
becomes your windy smile...
i'll stay with you a while.

memories
have brought you here in sunlight,
while this misty day
i find a different way,

pondering
the patterns in my mind
to look through magic eyes
at ancient winter skies.

RENEGADE

this bullish gray cloud
rolled into my sky one day,
changed the color of it all,
it so heavy and ominous,
daring to block the light of the sun.

as if that weren't enough,
it grew and spread
like the most fertile substance
i'd ever seen
until some alien wind
had it roiling and boiling
up there in its darkened firmament.

as you might expect,
it busted loose,
released its mad torrent,
battered peaks and vales alike,
chased the winged creatures
into their hidden lairs.

and I had to take inside
my sunshine plans
for another day
like laundry that might never dry.

the pre-evening calm
brought me out the door
to squeak my feet
in the rainsoaked grass.

and wouldn't you know?
that fat-head cloud
still lurked over the hills,
enjoying its ornery chuckle
to keep us wondering.
and then through some alchemy

of our Gaian atmosphere
or angle of the nodding sun,
silvered rays came down in rivers,
danced upon the new-washed forests.

spellpound there i was;
dazzled witness to that renegade,
that bullish gray cloud
now director of the light

kingpin in that sky's creation,
thief of midday's verdent colors,
once destroyer of my plans,
now gifter of transcendent vision.

LIGHT-SHOWER

i've seen the stars of the morning
before the sun climbed the lip of the earth.
the lights from millions of years ago
shone through the lens of the present
though having, eons before, exploded into the void.

i've seen the stars of the morning,
before the mountain's profile could be found
to trace the sky with its sacred line,
during early chores before my long workday,
rubbing sleep from my eyes in the morning chill.

i've seen the stars of the morning
while bearing my son's heavy wet worn jeans,
oblivious to the weight; pinning damp clothes
onto the lines with intuitive braille,
becoming clean, along with laundry, in star-shine.

i've seen the stars of the morning,
one breaking loose with a long blue trail...
were you there as well during that phenomenon,
outside your door to watch the golden dawn,
one with me, so far away, awakened?

92

REQUITED LOVE

there is a sound but no cause.
it's like the memory of wind sighing,
like the feel of your moan against my cheek.
the sound courses in my mind,
writing the scores of new love.

there is a vision with no light.
from whence do you come in the darkened room?
your eyes impale me upon your need,
your skin washes temptingly before me
as your hand beckons me to you.

there is flame without spark,
just as hope began to die alone,
convicting me as an outcast of love...
rising up between us full-blown hot
to sear us long before we are prepared.

there is truth with mute voice,
clear transmission in the temple room
like we two are a crystal bell
struck just so by emptiness
so that our forms find their release.

HER ANTIDOTE FOR BLUES

on knees i scrub the tiles
my face alight with smiles
the baby screams next door
the mom can take no more
i ruffle up her hair
and nestle her right there
against my heart so warm
she stills her infant storm
her eyes enormous blue
gaze into mine right through

the boy across the way
cranks up his rock to play
that dreadful deaf'ning boom
allows no one the room
to think or concentrate
yet joy dwells at my gate
and lingers through my day
though difficult the way
with monumental tasks
how can you smile? he asks
the reasons? there are two
for i am loved by you
and there at your right hand
i find that i can stand

to face reality
with equanimity
moreover you and i
in harmony apply
tremendous skillful means
with knowledge unforeseen
to practice transformation
to nurture realization
& thus the mind's brought home
it's wisdom we do own
to view illusions right
transforming dark to light
and acts of ill intent
into enlightenment

EPILOGUE

The light of awareness fills the vast empty space of your unfolding being
Lifting you into renewed realization of the preciousness of This Now.

With gratitude to Padmasambhava for the guidance of illumined mind

A surprise for a young author --
NORI CRIST

DEER

gentle one
she is soft
four very hard feet
beautiful

PICKET FENCES

When we were small a picket fence was customary.
Some were painted white and some plain wood.
For us kids it was a test to see who could walk it best,
and if we walked it, well, we knew that we were good.

Picket fences are made from picket slats,
nailed to 2 X 4's; some are pointed, some are flat.
Al Ferguson's fence was tall and had the skinniest pickets of all.
We felt like Walenda's if we managed to walk that.

There's a comparison to draw about that 2 x 4.
Where we placed one foot ahead each shaky step.
And the changes in our lives now that we're husbands or wives
and the decisions that we make now we're grown up.

With every step we take there's a chance that we might break,
there's a chance that we may stumble or may fall.
But when we gain our balance, we give ourselves a new chance
to succeed and that's the greatest thing of all.

If it's fences when we're kids, or decisions when we're big,
we're the only ones who know we've done our best.
If we land upon our seat, or land upon our feet
the attempt is a sure measure of success.

KEEP MOVING

We're all gone die. Hell, we're dying!
No use sitting there moping, crying.
Get up! Start something. Get it done.
Learn a lesson. Have some fun!
Plan a little for tomorrow. It's pretty far away.
Hold on loosely to the past. That was yesterday.
What you give out's what you get.
If you ain't seen millions yet
Keep right on giving.
You're still living.

COMPANION

Once, I sat beside a rock.
It was the most
companionable rock
I ever knew.

We sat together.
Silently.
As rocks and people
sometimes do.

The wind sang us
its life song.
Unaware of us as they passed,
a doe and fawn.

An aged pine tree danced
its silent, ageless dance.
The rock and I,
we sat entranced.

Together we watched
the sun go down.
Then I drove
back to town.

QUERY OF A POET'S TALE

I want to be a writer
So I write
Does this mean I'm a writer?
A housewife's notes
Don't make a poem
But every note
Sets a tone
Receiving ears
Can make it clear
What one has said
What have I said?
It seems worth a mention
That I could be
A poet
And think in phrases
Filling pages
Gripping the moment
Right now, unfolding
With ink to the page
Photons and neurons
Relay the tale
Replaying a trail
Of oft-repeated themes
I think I could be a poet
Write phrases
Instead of pages
Retire early and ponder
Imaginative things
Like numbers and forces
And others' ideals
Now perchance
I think like a poet
But phrases or pages
Are just phases and stages
Detailing the type of growing
To do
If I'm to be a poet

ILLUMINE BEINGS

Potential
Illumine Beings
Resistance
Illumine Beings
Riding light with impulsion
To flow
Is not to know
What comes next
While doing this
A flutter of joy
Transfer of light
Connection to being
Currency value

POEM IN A PASTURE

Stop and notice
You are
Take time
Enough
Digest your now
Invest in spontaneous
Right action
Secure and unknowing
Breathing, respiration
Unconsciously constant
Heartbeats repeated
Pacing the day

WRITER'S RESONANCE

A pause to write
Right away
Resonance registering
A leaf
    leave it alone
A sound
    sound it out
A story
    store it away
But oh!
To grasp more than a phrase
More than a glimpse
At the upcoming page

A pause to write
For a chance to record
That pulsing core
To which
The rest of life
Is only an analogy